Memories Of An Adopted Child

Memories Of An Adopted Child

Christine Carol Meakin

Library of Congress Control Number: 2015914832
ISBN: Hardcover   978-1-5144-6153-2
               Softcover   978-1-5144-6152-5
               eBook   978-1-5144-6151-8

Print information available on the last page.

Rev. date: 10/02/2015

To order additional copies of this book, contact:
Xlibris
800-056-3182
www.Xlibrispublishing.co.uk
Orders@Xlibrispublishing.co.uk
718303

CONTENTS

Memories of an Adopted Child

This book is dedicated to my adoptive parents Louisa and George Bossons to thank them for giving me a wonderful life!

December 1944

The birth of a daughter is a joyous occasion to be celebrated happily. However, if this child is your second daughter and the first one has been adopted, then the situation becomes more complex.

Preface

My mother was a young single girl who came over to England from Ireland at the beginning of the 1940s. She was accompanied by her younger sister, and together they wanted a better life and to live and work in London. They had another sister who was already working there, training to be a nurse.

Eventually they both obtained work in a public house called the Greyhound near Hammersmith. The work was hard, but they began to build a life for themselves and made friends.

When I try to imagine what life was like in those war years, it seems difficult to know how my mother felt and adapted to life in London. Was she homesick? She had lived all her life in a tiny village in County Leitrim and was brought up in a Catholic family with two brothers and four sisters.

I was to find out much later in my life that this was where my mother and father met. He owned the Greyhound, so he was her employer. He was married with a daughter.

CHAPTER 1

My Early Years

I realised as a small happy child that I was different from my friends—not in looks, belongings, religion, clothes, or toys, but I knew in the way small children often do that I was in some way unique.

We lived in a small mining area in a semi-detached house which was situated at the edge of the village.

Everybody knew everybody in the village, and of course, everyone attended the Methodist chapel. Sunday school was a must, and we all enjoyed the Sunday school anniversaries, prize-giving, and Sunday school outings.

The differences were subtle and often beyond my understanding. I knew, for example, that my mum and dad were much older than my friends' parents. Also their mothers didn't work, but mine did. I attended a nursery school, but they didn't. I had no brothers or sisters, and probably because of the nursery school, I could read and write at a very early age. I was also given piano lessons, which was extremely unusual.

At the age of four and a half, I started at a Church of England primary school where I met a girl called Judy. She was of mixed race, which was rare at the time, and she was the only mixed-race child I had ever seen. We immediately became firm friends, and I did not realise at the time that this was to be the most important friendship of both our lives!

Our birthdays are six days apart, and we are Sagittarians. Our friendship and lives have been intertwined for sixty-five years with an inexplicable bond felt by both of us, and this still continues to this day. On my seventieth birthday, I received a card from Judy with the following words: 'To my dear friend, where have all the years gone? I look back to when we were two hopeful teenagers and your mum was making us laugh while we were knitting in your front room.'

I remember quite clearly the night that I found out that I was adopted. My dad was a miner, and like all the other men, he went for a drink at the local pub in the evenings. This would leave Mum and me to listen to the radio or play cards and ludo. Quite often, Mum would be knitting or making me doll's clothes. There was no such thing as television.

We always enjoyed Saturday evenings when Mum would be cooking the roast with roast potatoes for Sunday lunch. Supper would be a sandwich of hot roast beef with a roast potato. We would always listen to the radio because on the Light Programme would be a play called *Saturday Night Theatre*. It was the highlight of the week!

One particular night, I was chattering away and talking about Judy. I suddenly asked Mum why Judy was black and had fuzzy hair when her mum and dad looked different. Her reaction was completely out of character for my mum because she suddenly found something to do in the kitchen and pretended that she hadn't heard the question. Of course, this didn't put me off at all, and I promptly repeated the question. She then said that Judy had been adopted when she was a baby. I sat and digested this information for a while, and then for no reason, I suddenly said, 'Was I adopted then?' Mum immediately went back into the kitchen, rattling some dishes.

I waited for her to come back into the living room, and I could tell that she was upset. Her face was red, and she looked quite stressed. None of these made any sense to me, so I asked again, and she looked at me and just said, 'Yes!'

It was as if time stood still at that moment. I never expected that answer, and for a moment, I didn't know what to say. Of course, that moment didn't last long, and I bombarded Mum with loads of questions. I certainly wasn't upset. I was quite excited. I had a lovely mum and dad and lived in a happy home, so there were no problems, but I was very interested in how this had happened.

Chapter 2

The Beginnings of My Background

My mum sat down and took a deep breath. I was agog with apprehension. She told me that she and my dad were never lucky enough to have children but had always wanted them. Then when they had the chance to adopt a baby, they were really happy and agreed to have me straight away. They loved me very much, she said, and I was everything to them.

I asked many more questions, but that was all she was prepared to tell me at the time. She was also aware it was nearly time for my dad to come home.

I went to school the next day, full of excitement. I told everybody!

For the next few months, life went on normally, and I put it to the back of my mind. However, one evening I was out playing with my friends when an older girl who lived near to us said that she knew who my real mother was.

She said that two little girls who attended Sunday school with us were my sisters. I knew them, of course, but I didn't know who their mother was. I never thought any more of this because I was sure that my real mother was a princess or an actress or even a singer!

One of my friends who was playing with us and heard all this conversation was my cousin Pauline. I didn't realise that she would go home and repeat all this to my auntie Emmie, who was Mum's sister-in-law.

The next day, when I arrived home from school, Mum was sitting in the front room window, looking out. I went in and asked if I could go out to play as usual, and she said I had to wait a while because she was looking for someone. I realised that she had been crying and asked her why she was upset. She then told me that Auntie Emmie had been to see her and told her about this other girl telling me who my real mother was. She was waiting to see her to tell her how annoyed she was! I was terrified! I didn't want Mum to confront this girl because she was older than me and I didn't want a fallout with her. Also she was a bit of a bully, and I certainly didn't want to get on her wrong side!

I went up to Mum, and putting my arms round her, I said I couldn't care less about anybody else. I loved her and that was all that mattered. I begged her not to speak to this girl, and so of course, she didn't in the end. We went back in the living room, and she said that when Dad went out after tea, she would tell me everything. I didn't really want to go out to play or even have any tea, but I knew that I had to be patient so that she would tell me.

Chapter 3

The Start of My Journey

As I said previously, my dad was a miner and had a drink in the local pub with the other men. One Sunday afternoon, he came home from the pub and had his Sunday dinner, as it was called in those days. (It was never Sunday lunch!) After finishing his dinner, he went to bed for an afternoon nap as usual, and my mum started to soak some washing, ready for the next day.

There was a knock at the back door. She went to answer it, and there stood my real mother with me in her arms. Of course, my mum knew who she was and the circumstances of my birth, but she tried not to appear too surprised at this unusual visit. My mum invited her in and made her welcome as I know she would have. My mother placed me on the settee and accepted a cup of tea. She came straight to the point of her visit; she told my mum that the man whose house she was lodging in had come home from the pub and said that he had been talking to my dad at lunchtime. My dad had said that he and my mum had always wanted a child but had never been lucky enough. She explained that she couldn't afford to keep me and asked my mum if she wanted me.

My mum was an intelligent woman and thought this through carefully. Of course, she wanted me but was sceptical of my mother's motives. She said that she would only take me if it was done legally and she would go to court for me to be adopted. My mother agreed to this and said that she would probably return to Ireland in the future so she would never have anything to do with me or see me. She also agreed that she would never approach me or speak to me in the future.

With this agreement, my mum said yes, and my mother got up to go home. She left me on the settee, and Mum said, 'Are you leaving her now?' Mother said yes. My mum was flabbergasted as she had nothing for a baby and it was Sunday, when all the shops were closed! However, she wasn't about to argue and just said that that was fine.

My mother left, and my mum went upstairs two at a time to get my dad up out of bed. He came downstairs, rubbing his eyes, and asked whose baby I was. Mum said, 'She's ours!'

Then the reality of the situation hit them both. Obviously, I would need feeding and a cot to sleep in! My mother had explained that I never had a cot. I just slept between her and the wife of the couple that she was lodging at. My dad immediately went into the kitchen and got a drawer out of the wooden dresser. They lined it with a blanket and sheet and placed me in it. Next, old towels and tea clothes were ripped up to make nappies until the next day, when they could buy some. Mum said the lady up the road was selling a pram, but Dad said that, of all things, I should have a new pram and he would buy it!

But the worst thing they were up against was that I needed feeding. I was only three months old, and they had no bottles or teats or in fact any baby milk. In those days, you could only get tins of National Dried Milk. So in desperation, they heated some ordinary milk in a saucepan. They propped me up on a cushion, and each had a teaspoon and fed me the warm milk. I can only imagine how they coped that afternoon. Mum was a very private person, and she would have never asked anyone for help!

The next day, my mum went to the local town by tram to get my new pram. My auntie Edith used to leave my cousin Keith with Mum when she went to work, and so when she came to the house, she helped Mum look after me and would take me with her while she went on her shopping trip. My cousin Keith clearly remembers the day when he saw a new baby in my mum's house.

The thing my mum did was to visit the district nurse/midwife, who only lived up the road from us. She told her everything, and the nurse was most sympathetic and told my mum how to go about arranging my adoption. She also told my mum she had delivered me and that I was not my mother's first child! This comment was to prove crucial in later years!

My natural mother was as good as her word and attended the adoption hearing, which was held approximately two months later in a nearby town. I was left at home with my auntie Edith and Keith. Mum and Dad went on the bus to the hearing. The awful thing was that my mother had to also travel on the same bus! After the hearing, as Mum and Dad were leaving the court, my mother was walking behind them. My mum felt that she couldn't just walk past her without saying anything, so she just said, 'Thank you. You've made me the happiest woman in the world!'

The next problem was catching the bus back to the village. They would all be travelling together again! So my dad said they would splash out on a taxi. This solved the problem somewhat, but as they travelled past the bus stop, my natural mother was there waiting for the bus. My mum looked at her, and she was crying!

After we had this talk, Mum said how hard it had been with everyone in the village knowing about it. Of course, I never realised until years later just how hard it had been for them. My mum and dad were both in their forties and had never had any children of their own. What a shock to suddenly have the full responsibility of this three-month-old baby without any time to prepare anything for it or without any outside support or help.

CHAPTER 4

Life Goes On

I discussed all this information with my friends, who thought it was very exciting. Many times we would go past my mother's house just to look at her, and when I saw her, I realised how much I resembled her in looks. I also continued to see my two half-sisters at Sunday school, but I never spoke to them.

I was always aware that at every Sunday school anniversary, I was extremely well dressed, with new shoes and coat and a new dress to wear on the stage to sing in front of the congregation. Of course, now I understand that my natural mother would be part of the congregation, and my mum would want me to look my best. My hair would be carefully put in 'rags' on Saturday night so that I had lovely ringlets for Sunday.

One Sunday, I was going home from Sunday school with my friend, and we had to call at her grandma's house. While we were there, her grandma looked at me, then turned to my friend's mum and said, 'My goodness, she looks just like her mother, doesn't she?'

I mentioned this to my mum, and I could see she was upset as she went into the kitchen to prepare dinner. It never dawned on me as a child the meaning behind this comment. All I thought was that my hair was dark brown and my mum's was ginger!

Another unusual thing I remember is that quite often I wasn't invited to friends' birthday parties. I never knew why, and it wasn't all the time, but I suppose people then were prejudiced about an adopted child. There could have been a stigma attached to it, especially living in such a small village. I also remember once at Sunday school sports, we had a running race; I came first, but the woman judging said I was second. I knew I'd won, and my best friend also said I was first. But the woman ignored me, and the girl who won had the first prize, which was a fairy doll! I was heartbroken, and to this day, I've never got over that injustice.

My mum never commented on it, but Auntie Edith and Uncle Stuart would take me out on their motorbike and sidecar with my cousin Keith. I loved these trips out; they were wonderful. I remember once we had been to Sherwood Forest and had a picnic there. Keith and I climbed trees, and it was very hot. On the way back, it began to thunder and lighten, and rain poured down. Uncle Stuart took us to a pub to dry off, then we went to the cinema. All I remember is that the film was about a boxer, but I loved every minute of it!

CHAPTER 5

The Early Years at School

My primary school was a Church of England school, and I had to travel on the bus because it wasn't the nearest school. My mum didn't like the nearest school and wanted me to go to a different school. I was happy, and of course, Judy was there. One day we were having dancing lessons, and when the headmaster came into the lesson, we were told to carry on dancing. When I looked around, the headmaster had a visitor with him, a man in a smart suit. As I looked, they were both looking at me, and I thought I must be doing the dance wrong, so I tried to concentrate more. But they were still talking to my teacher, and I felt embarrassed because I knew they were talking about me.

I forgot all about this incident until I went home. I ran in to ask my mum if I could go out to play and the same man was sitting on our settee and Mum had her posh voice on. The man asked me if I was happy, and of course, I said, 'Yes, very.' I was then told by Mum to go out to play. To this day, I have no idea who this man was, and I never asked my mum about it, but I wonder now if he may have been a social worker or someone just checking if I was okay.

So many instances happened when I wished I had asked my mum, but I was always conscious of perhaps upsetting her. My dad would never ever talk about me being adopted. I soon learned that this was a no-go area. He absolutely denied that I was adopted and said it wasn't for discussion and that I was theirs, end of subject! He was such a lovely man. He never told me off or disciplined me in any way. I could get away with anything with him and quite often did!

I was always aware that we weren't wealthy and that Mum had to go to work for extra money. However, we had a holiday every year usually with Auntie Edith, Uncle Stuart, and Keith. Sometimes my granddad would also be with us. Keith and I are very close, and I love him like a brother. Keith was a sensitive child and sometimes shy, but he always looked after me. Most holidays were spent at Rhyl in North Wales. We would rent a bungalow at a place called Sandy Cove. At night Keith and I were allowed to catch the bus to go to the Amusement Arcade at Marine Lake. It was amazing! The slot machines were the old penny ones, and we usually had about two shillings between us to spend. This was twenty-four pennies and kept us entertained all evening.

The days were always spent on the beach. I remember when it was getting dark, sometimes Uncle Stuart would take Keith and me up to the beach to build a wall of stones, then we would go up the next morning to see how the tide had demolished it.

As I grew up, I realised that Auntie Edith couldn't walk properly and often used a walking stick. It seemed that she wasn't getting any better, so I decided to ask my mum about it, and she told me that Auntie Edith had multiple sclerosis. I didn't know then how serious this was.

Then when I was about eight, the house next door to us became available to rent, and to my delight, Auntie Edith, Uncle Stuart, and Keith moved in. This was wonderful because now I could always go out in the motorbike and sidecar! On very rare occasions, I was allowed to sit behind Uncle Stuart on the pillion of the bike. What a treat! But this didn't happen often as this was always Keith's place.

At the age of eleven, I passed my eleven-plus examination to go to a grammar school, and Judy passed as well. This was really unusual in our village, and my mum was over the moon about it and really proud. I wasn't convinced at the time that this was a good thing because none of my other friends were going to a grammar school, and I hated being different because I knew I was different! The other thing was that Judy and I didn't go to the same grammar school and you had to accept the place that you were offered. Also you were automatically referred to as a snob!

None of this nonsense from me deterred my mum. She was determined that I would go and have the best education I could get. She was worried about the cost of my uniform, but fate took a hand, and sadly, my granddad died. One day I overheard a conversation between my mum and Auntie Edith in which they were discussing granddad's will. There were eleven children, and they all received thirty-two pounds! This, of course, was a considerable amount of money in the early 1950s. Mum spent it all on getting my school uniform!

The school which I attended was called Clayton Hall Grammar School, and I loved it! I was so nervous on my first day, but the school was an old hall in beautiful grounds with a wood and orchards. I remember one summer we were allowed to go to the wood for one of our English lessons. We were doing Shakespeare's *A Midsummer Night's Dream*, and we all sat on the grass or tree stumps, reading the play.

I still went to Sunday school every Sunday, and I played the piano for the hymn singing. When I was fifteen, I became friends with a girl from the new housing estate in the village, and she had lots of friends and was very popular. Her name was Ann. She invited me to their house, and she had a brother and two sisters. I made friends with all her friends, and we all went around together, sometimes going to the cinema or church activities but, most importantly, the Friday night youth club. This was the highlight of the week. It was then that I met a boy called Stuart Meakin, whom I had known from the village. I really fancied him and thought he was the most handsome boy I had ever met. However, he didn't feel the same way as me, so I just had to worship him in silence!

My school years passed by so quickly, and I was lucky enough to gain five O-level subjects. I kept in touch with all my classmates, and we still have reunions now. It saddens me when I hear of bullying in schools. I never ever saw anything of that nature in my school and indeed never knew what it was.

CHAPTER 6

Teenage Years

The Friday night youth club was still my favourite activity, and when I had finished all my exams, I was allowed to go away for a week to Blackpool with my friends. The best thing was that Stuart was going as well.

We stayed in a 'boarding house' near the north end of Blackpool; it was very basic, but it seemed to me like Buckingham Palace because Stuart was there. Of course, in those times, all the girls slept in one room, and all the boys in the other. We often played cards in one of the rooms in the evening. I shared a double bed with Kathy, one of the girls, and one night after having a wash and putting on my nightdress, I got into bed only to find there was itching powder on the sheets! It was awful. We were both itching like mad and had to dab cold water over our legs to relieve the itching. Everyone was laughing the next morning, and the main suspect we thought was Stuart, but no one admitted to doing it.

I was glad to be on holiday because I knew I had finished all my exams. During the week, I received a letter from my mum telling me to relax and enjoy myself because she knew how hard I'd tried. I wish I still have that letter!

The week went so fast, and I remember writing in my diary that I didn't know how I would live without seeing Stuart every day. How dramatic you can be at sixteen.

My first job when I left school was working in a chartered accountant's office as a junior. While I was still at school, I had previously worked in Woolworths on a Saturday and during school holidays; although it was tiring work, I did enjoy it. I was still friends with Judy, and we would go out together or, more usually, just listen to records in each other's houses. I would always be talking about Stuart, and we would be discussing the merits of other boys too.

My cousin Keith had a birthday party for his twenty-first birthday, and it was held at the King William, our local public house. Judy and I were both invited, and I can remember Judy's mum and dad making her a green two-piece suit for her to go in. I wore a lilac dress with matching beads. We thought we looked very smart. The party was amazing and carried on at my auntie's house, which of course was next door to ours. Judy's dad came to fetch her, and she was most put out about this even though it was one o'clock in the morning. Keith was seeing my friend Barbara at the time, and she said on her way home, 'I might never see him again!' We both laughed because she only lived six houses up the road. We didn't realise then that they would eventually get married.

CHAPTER 7

My Nursing Career

My job at the chartered accountant's began to get boring, and it was the same thing most days. I enjoyed working with the other audit clerks mostly because they were all boys! I learned a fast way of adding numbers up in columns, which I still use to this day. This was long before the use of calculators and adding machines.

One day one of the boys had a nosebleed which was quite bad and looked horrific. I got some cold water on a towel and held it on the bridge of his nose until it stopped bleeding, which it eventually did.

When I got home that night, I told my mum about it, and she said that she thought I would make a good nurse. The idea really interested me, and I knew that Judy had applied for nursing, so I asked her about it. She said she had got all the required books but she wasn't that keen any more and was trying to get into social services.

I wrote and applied to the local hospital, which was the City General Hospital, Stoke-on-Trent in Staffordshire. Judy gave me all the books and even a new pair of black lace-up shoes.

I was accepted for my nurse training, and I began in the preliminary training school (PTS) in April 1964. I had to live in at the hospital, and I had my own room, which was very cosy. I made loads of friends, and we enjoyed the hard work, especially night duty. We worked a forty-eight-hour week, but of course, it was always more than that because you never went off duty until you were told to by the ward sister. If she was busy, you carried on until she told you to go.

The training was a three-year course of very hard work. On my first ward, I was told to bed-bath this patient who was a man. I had never ever seen a man without his clothes on before. I had never seen my mum or dad undressed, only my mum in her nightdress and dressing gown! Luckily, I was with a senior nurse, who told me in no uncertain terms what to do. I have never sweat so much or been so embarrassed. I was eighteen at the time!

However, I overcame my shyness and got used to seeing anything. I smile when I think back how innocent I must have been.

The three years passed so quickly, and I began revising for my final exams to become a state-registered nurse. On the night before I took my written exam, I stayed at home, so I travelled to work on the bus the next day. When I got on the bus, the only seat available was next to my mother, who was sitting by herself.

Over the years, I had occasionally seen my natural mother in the village and also my two half-sisters.

I didn't want to be rude, so I smiled and sat beside her. She said hello, and so did I. She was obviously as embarrassed as I was, and she asked me if I was on my way to work. I told her I was doing my final exams, and she wished me good luck. I don't remember much more of our conversation, but I know she kept looking at me.

I passed my exams and was lucky enough to achieve the gold medal for Best Nurse of the Year. It was a prestigious award, and my mum and dad had to attend prize-giving and have tea with the matron. There was also a reporter from the local newspaper who took my photograph, and it was printed together with a write-up. Years later, I found out that my mother had cut the picture out of the newspaper and saved it!

CHAPTER 8

Finding Out More of My Beginnings

My nurse training took many and varied twists and turns in my life. I eventually did become engaged to Stuart Meakin, who by this time was in the army in the Royal Engineers, and for a time, we were very happy. I got on well with his family and especially his mum, who suffered from terrible leg ulcers; walking was difficult for her. She told me one day that she had been the one who suggested my Christian name to my mother.

At the time when I was born, my mother was lodging in the house across from Stuart's mum, who decided to go across and visit the new baby. She asked my mother what she was going to call me, and she replied that she hadn't yet decided. Apparently, because it was near to Christmas, the radio was playing carols, so Stuart's mum said, 'Why don't you call her Christmas Carol?'

So in the end, I was called Christine Carol. My mum changed me from being called Christine to being called Carol just to be different. So all my life, I have been called Carol except in official and hospital notes, where I use both names.

I was very content with my romance with Stuart. We got on so well, and I loved his brothers and sisters. We would often sit together on Sunday afternoons after dinner, playing cards. If Stuart was home for a forty-eight-hour pass, he would have to go back late on Sunday evening to his barracks. His dad would go with us on the bus, and after saying goodbye to Stuart, his dad would then take me home.

We still kept in touch with all our friends. Judy by this time was also courting, as it was called in those days.

Stuart and I were arranging the wedding, and we were going to live in Cyprus because Stuart had been posted out there for three years. I had never travelled any further than England, and I was very apprehensive, especially about leaving my mum.

Once again, as has so often happened in my life, fate decided to intervene, and I met someone else. Stuart was heartbroken and got special leave from the army, but I'd made my mind up, and I made probably one of my worst decisions of my life and would not make it up with him. This would be 1965. My mum and dad did everything they could to make me change my mind. My mum kept saying that I would regret it.

The following year, Stuart's mum sadly died at the age of forty-six. It was very sudden and a shock to the village. My mum insisted that I attended the funeral! I really didn't want to because I knew that I would meet up with Stuart again. However, in those days, you didn't argue if your mum insisted, so I did go to the funeral, and I sat at the back of the church on my own. Of course, Stuart saw me, and we exchanged a look, but that was as far as it went.

I heard sometime later that Stuart had married.

CHAPTER 9

A Chance Meeting and a Sad Death

I married and was blessed in 1970 with the birth of a son, Robert Alexander. I was working in theatre at the time and took maternity leave, which meant that I went back to work when Robert was six weeks old. My mum and dad looked after him, and I remember my mum ringing me at work when he cut his first tooth.

One day my mum and I were shopping in the village, and Robert was in his pram. Mum and Dad had obviously bought his pram; it was a lovely cream-coloured one. We were chatting away to each other when I suddenly saw my mother walking towards us. There was no way of avoiding her, and I was so embarrassed. However, my mum took it all in her stride and spoke to her straight away. They stood together and, as far as I remember, discussed the weather. I just stood there wishing the ground would open up and swallow me.

Then my mum said, 'Would you like to see Robert?' and turned his covers back. My mother made a real fuss over him and said he was beautiful. She stood there for a few minutes just looking. I don't honestly remember saying anything at all. My mum did all the talking, and I wonder now all these years later how wonderful she was to do that! How many other women would be so selfless and kind as she was?

It was during the 1970s that the country was converted to North Sea Gas. This consisted of a team of gas fitters who came into your home and changed your gas appliances. One day I opened the door, and Stuart was standing there. He was the foreman of the gas fitters, and so he came in to do the work. We chatted and got on very well; it was a big temptation for both of us as we definitely still had feelings for each other. He did two more visits but sadly then had to move on.

The years went by, and in 1974, I gave birth to a daughter named Denise Lilian. My life was complete!

Then when Denise was nearly one, my mum had a stroke, and sadly, she died a few months later. I was with her when she died. I had been sitting by her bedside, holding her hand, and it was a warm night. I went to the restroom and sat there by the window when suddenly a warm, gentle breeze brushed by my cheek. I just knew it was the end. I rushed back to her bedside just as she took her last breath. It's hard to put into words all the emotions I felt. I just felt numb at the time, and it was like it wasn't real. My two aunties were with me, and they took me home afterwards. All I can say is that, on that night, I lost my best friend! You can never ever be prepared for the loss! I was thirty years old.

Now at seventy, I still cannot sing Christmas carols without crying. I get a lump in my throat and think of all the wonderful Christmases I had as a child. My mum once took me to the cinema when Keith's dog was hit by a car and I couldn't stop crying. We went to see *White Christmas* (with Bing Crosby and Rosemary Clooney). I cannot watch this film now even though I love it!

CHAPTER 10

A Visit from My Birth Mother

The death of my mum brought a new dimension to my life because suddenly my natural mother made an appearance.

I still had my dad, who lived nearby in a retirement bungalow but was very independent. He came to my house most days and especially all day on Sundays. He loved his grandchildren and always came on holidays with us.

I was working on nights in theatre at the time, but on one particular day, I was on a day off. The doorbell went, and when I opened the door, there was my mother. It was so unexpected, and I was so shocked to see her standing there. I invited her in, and straight away she apologised for just turning up like she had. Many things have been written about children meeting their birth mothers and all the emotion involved, but all I felt was acute embarrassment. I didn't know what to say or do!

I asked her to sit down, and she began to talk. She said she was sorry about my mum and what a lovely lady she had been. She then told me of the promise she'd made to my mum about never talking to me, but she wondered if now she could be part of my life. My head was going round in circles. I just kept hoping she wouldn't try to put her arms round me. I pulled myself together and said it would be okay but I could never call her mother. She said that she understood that perfectly and would be happy if I called her Agnes.

She said that she would answer any questions I wanted to ask her. I began by asking about who my father was, and she told me everything she knew. Her first comment to me was that I got my brains and intelligence from my father. She said that he came to England from Australia in the late 1930s. His name was Jack King. He was also a semi-professional boxer, and he owned the Greyhound pub, where they had met. She then made an odd comment about one of his hands. He used to make bets with the customers in the pub about a deep line which ran across the middle of his hand. He said that he'd never met anyone else with this peculiarity. I couldn't believe it. I showed her my hands, and I have this deep line in the centre of both of them. I also had never met anyone else with it. She was amazed and said how pleased he would have been. My son, Robert, also has a line on his right hand.

She told me that my father was a Roman Catholic and would never leave his wife, so her only option when she knew she was pregnant was to leave London and move to Stoke-on-Trent, where her sister Betty lived, and hopefully live with her for a while until I was born.

I asked if she had any photographs of him, and she said she had one but had thrown it away. I don't remember feeling disappointed because no one could have replaced my dad.

She then said that she would like us to keep in touch and she understood how I must feel towards her but she loved me and I was her flesh and blood. Truth to be told, I didn't feel anything at all, but I was polite and said I would meet up with her occasionally. She said that she had regretted having me adopted and could never listen to any programmes on the radio about adoption.

Another thing she said to me was that, after her first husband (the father of my two half-sisters) died, she had met the man whom she was now married to. She had taken him to the local club, and someone said to her, 'Are you going to tell him about Carol?' She said she felt annoyed with this person because people never forget the past! I felt annoyed that she'd said that because what did she expect living in such close proximity to me?

She got up to leave, and I began to panic. I stood as far away from her as possible without being rude so that she wouldn't try to put her arm round me or kiss me. In any event, she didn't, and she took my telephone number and said she would ring me from time to time.

When she'd gone, I had to sit down to gather my thoughts because I just didn't know how to feel. I wished I still had my mum so I could talk to her about it, but then I knew I wouldn't have been able to talk to her without upsetting her. There was absolutely no way I could discuss this with my dad!

CHAPTER 11

The Death of My Birth Mother

Over the next few years, Agnes and I began to form a friendship. She met Robert and Denise and began to send them birthday cards, but they were always just plain ones. Robert accepted who she was and didn't really have an opinion about her, but Denise would never accept it and got quite angry sometimes because, in her young eyes, things were very black and white! Her favourite saying was 'She left you on a doorstep!' No amount of explaining that this was not true would stop her from saying it!

I also met both my half-sisters, who seemed very nice, but I had nothing in common with them, and they obviously didn't really want anything to do with me. I also met two of my aunties, Betty and Mary. They were lovely, and I loved them straight away. Auntie Mary was the sister who was a nurse, and I resembled her even more than Agnes. She had two daughters, Annette and Monica. They were so lovely towards me, and I felt a real affection for them, which has developed over the years; we now have a natural family bond. I also met Jimmy, who was Auntie Betty's son, and he had married a girl named Pauline, whom I used to go to school with.

I was working in a nursing home by this time and still had my dad, who was ninety years old and still active.

One day I had a phone call at work from the youngest of my half-sisters, who said that her mum was ill in the hospital with her diabetes and asked whether I wanted to go to visit her. Of course, I said yes and found out which ward she was on at the hospital.

The following day, I went to visit Agnes on my own. Robert, who was nursing at the time, said he would also pop in to see her. She was sitting up on the bed with her foot on a stool; apparently, she'd got some infection in it, which was causing her problems.

I sat with her, and we talked about everything. She said how pleased she was that I had come to visit her. I decided there and then that I was going to be brave and ask her the question which had been in my mind since we'd become friends. I asked her if she'd had a baby before she had me. She looked at me and said no. I said that my mum told me that the district nurse had said I wasn't her first child. Agnes just said that my mum must've got it wrong. But I said to her that my mum had never lied to me about anything. She said again that she must have got it wrong.

I let it drop at that because I could see she wasn't well and was tired, so I took my leave and said I would be back soon. I still didn't kiss her. I often wished now that I had done so.

She died the following day, and I went to the hospital where she was still on the ward. One of my half-sisters asked me if I wanted to see her, and I said yes. She let me in behind the screens and left me alone with Agnes. I stood there for a moment, looking at the woman who had given birth to me, and then I bent down and kissed her!

CHAPTER 12

Finding Out about My Sister

I attended Agnes's funeral together with Robert and Denise. It was rather awkward because, as her eldest child, the undertaker asked me to walk in first behind the coffin. I knew I should be crying as the others were doing, but I just couldn't do it. She was a nice lady whom I was friends with, but she wasn't my mum. Nothing can change this fact.

After the funeral, Pauline invited me to go to her house for a drink together with Auntie Betty. Robert and Denise had gone back to work. I remember it was a warm day, and we sat outside in the garden, chatting.

The next day was a Saturday, and in the morning, I had a phone call from Pauline, who sounded a little upset. She asked if she could come to see me as soon as possible and that it was important. I waited for her to arrive, and I remember hoping that Auntie Betty wasn't ill or anything like that.

Pauline came, and her daughter Jayne was with her. She sat down and didn't waste any time. She said that, after I left the previous day, Auntie Betty had told her that she had kept a secret for Agnes for many years but felt she couldn't keep it any longer. I had an older sister! I just knew, and Pauline could see that I wasn't surprised. I told her about what my mum had always said.

Pauline told Betty that they had to tell me, and reluctantly Betty agreed. She didn't know many details except that she was roughly two years older than me and had been adopted through Hammersmith's social services. Betty thought that my father had arranged for her to be adopted by an employee at the Greyhound.

All I could think about was that I must find her. I was conscious of my age being well into my fifties, and I hoped that she was alive and well.

I didn't own a computer or have access to the Internet at the time, so I tried to think long and hard how to go about tracing someone.

I began with directory enquiries and got the telephone number of Hammersmith's social services. I spoke to a gentleman who listened to my story and was most sympathetic. He told me that even if he had any information, under the existing laws, there was no legislation to allow siblings any access to information. It was just for birth mothers trying to trace children and children trying to trace birth mothers. He did, however, give me the telephone number of an organisation called NORCAP, who often could help adopted people. He also mentioned the Salvation Army.

In the following weeks, Auntie Betty remembered that, a few years previously, she had seen an advert in the *Irish Times* from someone trying to trace Agnes. This was obviously my sister, and at the time, she lived in St Albans and gave an address. As far as Auntie Betty knew, this was never followed up, and I found the head office for that newspaper was in London near where my cousin Annette lived.

I rang Annette, and she thought it would be a good idea for me to ask permission to go through the archives at the newspaper office. I got the number and rang them, and they were more than happy to facilitate this request. So I set off to drive to London together with my daughter, Denise; Auntie Mary also offered to meet us there and help us with the search. We all arrived and the newspaper office made us comfortable and we began to trawl through the old papers. We were hot in that little room, but we carried on searching. Sadly it was all to no avail; we didn't find anything.

We went back to Annette's house and had a lovely meal before setting off back to Stoke-on-Trent.

I rang NORCAP but got nowhere although they were helpful and gave me the telephone number of the National Adoption Register.

In the meantime, Annette contacted the registry for births, marriages, and deaths in London. She found a copy of my sister's birth certificate, which we were able to purchase. This now meant that I knew her name, which was Deanna, and her date of birth. I remember when the birth certificate came through the post; I just stood with it in my hands, thinking, 'She does exist!'

Now I was determined. I wouldn't stop until I found her!

I then decided to ring the National Adoption Register for advice, and they sent me a very detailed form to fill in. They also said that, even if my sister was on the register, they wouldn't tell me. What they would do would be to contact her with the information, then it would be up to her to contact me. I completed the form and sent it back to them.

Nothing happened for a few weeks. Then one day, I was helping out in my daughter's flower shop, and I was feeling quite deflated about everything. It was quiet in the shop, and I thought I would ring the Adoption Register again.

I got through and spoke to a lovely girl who was very sympathetic and said that it could take a while to process all the information. For some unknown reason, I burst into tears on the phone and said, 'I've lived all my life without my sister, and she doesn't even know I exist.' The girl then said that she would verify some points with me and if she had time she would start a trace that very afternoon.

I finished at the flower shop at lunchtime, and I went home to get changed as I was on duty at the nursing home in the afternoon. As I went through the front door, the telephone rang. I picked it up, and it was the girl from the Adoption Register. She said she just wanted to know some more details about my sister, but the things she asked were the things I had already told her previously. There was something different about her voice, and all of a sudden, I just knew. I said, 'You've found her, haven't you?' She then said that she wasn't allowed to say. I begged her, but she was most professional and said she was optimistic.

I went to work in a daze! If I was right, I could be hearing from my sister soon. I knew that they would have to write to her, and then it would be her decision if she wanted to contact me.

It was exactly two days later when I got the phone call from her! Of course, I was at work, but she left a message on my answerphone, and she sounded lovely. I played it over and over again. I rang her, and we must have talked for at least an hour. She lived in Doncaster and was married with two daughters. The most amazing thing was that one of her daughters was named Denise, just like my daughter! We exchanged addresses and agreed to send photographs to each other. Deanna asked me if our mother was still alive, and I had to tell her that she had sadly died. I felt so sorry that I had to be the one to tell her this.

We exchanged lots of photographs and got to have a good idea what we both looked like. Both of us love the colour red, and we enjoyed finding out all these things about each other.

We were going on holiday soon after the phone call, but Deanna and I agreed to meet up as soon as I got back. In the meantime, we rang each other every day, and I even rang her from Portugal, where we were on holiday.

CHAPTER 13

Meeting My Sister

We arranged to meet at my house. Deanna told me she had always been called Dee as it was much easier and she preferred it.

I was so excited when the day came, and the meeting was wonderful. We talked and talked over endless cups of tea. I couldn't believe how much she resembled our birth mother even though I had seen her photographs prior to our meeting. Another thing which I discovered at our meeting was that Dee had a deep line across her left hand. I explained to her the significance of this, and she was thrilled. We also had the same blood group of B positive.

Dee told me that she was a diabetic and that she had to take insulin. She had no idea she had inherited this condition from her mother.

Dee also said that she never knew that she was adopted. She had been brought up in Chelsea, but since her marriage, she had moved around with various occupations. She worked in the children's services when we met and had a very important job. She also did Ofsted inspections for schools, which entailed travelling around the country. She only found out that she was adopted when she needed her full birth certificate for a job application; when she applied, it was an adoption certificate. Her adoptive parents had passed away by this time, so she couldn't ask them any questions.

She managed to find the name of her birth mother and, from then on, had tried to trace her with no success.

I asked Dee if she would like to visit our mother's grave, and she said she would. We went in my car, just the two of us. It was only a short journey, but I wanted to have Dee to myself for a while without husbands. We drove to the churchyard, and we walked to the grave. We held hands while she just stood there quietly. I didn't know how Dee was feeling. I had been lucky enough to have always known Agnes, but Dee hadn't. I felt so sorry for her. As we drove away, I tentatively asked if she was all right, and she said she was and that she had said her goodbye silently while we were at the graveyard.

After our initial meeting, we became very close, and although we lived several miles apart, we rang each other every night. We often spent weekends at each other's houses and met our friends.

Dee also met our two half-sisters, Sandra and Eileen, Auntie Betty and Auntie Mary, and our cousins Jimmy, Annette, and Monica.

Dee and I decided that we would like to visit Ireland as neither of us had ever been. Auntie Betty said that she would take us and show us where our mother was born. We stayed at the local public house in the town of Mohill, which was near to another of our aunts named Bea. She made us very welcome and had already been told who we were. I imagine it was somewhat of a shock when she found out, but no one ever told us what was said. We had an amazing time in Ireland. We had flown to Dublin and then gone by train to Mohill. The scenery was beautiful and so green. I felt it was like stepping back in time.

The following day, we had a massive breakfast at the pub, and it was the first time I'd tasted soda bread; it was gorgeous. I had also tasted Guinness the previous night in the bar. We set off to see the remains of the farmhouse where they had all grown up. It seemed so tiny and, of course, just rubble now after all the years. The place was called Gort and was lovely; it is situated between the town of Mohill and the village of Dromod. I tried to imagine the whole family growing up together and being so close. I always envied large families.

I remember we also visited the village and also some friends of Auntie Betty's who were farmers. Each place was very liberal with tots of whiskey which I didn't refuse because I didn't want to offend anyone. Dee did the same. We felt quite tipsy at the end of our visits.

Auntie Bea was hilarious and really funny. I thought she was wonderful even though I struggled to understand her sometimes. Both the aunties had several disagreements over trivial things, and Dee and I found ourselves laughing so much.

When our trip was over, we actually felt that we were Irish. I have never met such friendly, warm people.

We were by now firmly sisters. Dee has two daughters and three grandchildren. My nieces are called Denise and Claire. Denise has three children called Terri, Kelly, and Tom.

They all attended Robert's wedding, and we had a real get-together. Another similarity which became obvious to us was how much Claire and Robert resembled each other. They could have definitely been brother and sister. However, Dee's Denise is the image of Agnes. I know that I look like her, but Denise does even more so.

Over the years, we have been to several places. We had a holiday together in Paris. It was Dee and I with Claire and my Denise; this was in 1998. We had our portraits sketched at Montmartre and generally had a lovely time.

We spent a weekend together in Newcastle upon Tyne. Dee had visited this hotel previously when she was doing an Ofsted inspection, and she had loved it, so she took us there. We also went shopping in Gateshead.

We both tried to get information on our father, but sadly, we never found anything. Dee's husband even wrote to Henry Cooper to see if there was anything in the boxing archives about a Jack King, but nothing came of it. All we know from Auntie Betty is that he was married when he met Agnes and he had a daughter called Sylvia.

CHAPTER 14

Journey's End

At the age of seventy, I now feel that I have come full circle with my life. All my earlier questions and uncertainties have now been answered and explained. I know how lucky I was to be adopted by two such wonderful people and to be brought up in a large extended adoptive family. I love all my cousins, and I know that they feel the same way towards me. Three of my cousins closest to me are Keith, Drinda, and Paul. Sadly, I lost Paul a few years ago in a motorbike accident. I think of him often and miss him greatly.

Of course, I have another family—my sister, Dee, my two half-sisters (one of whom I also lost due to illness), my two lovely nieces and their families, and my cousins Annette, Monica, and Jimmy. I love them dearly.

Many adopted children never find their birth parents. My friend Judy has tried over the years to trace hers, but although she made some progress with her birth mother, she never actually got to find her.

If I could send any message to adopted children, it would be to say that you are *not* a second-class citizen and that you *are* equally as good, if not better, than your peers. You were chosen. Your parents didn't have to have you; they wanted you!

If you do try to find your birth parents, be prepared for every eventuality. Always remember that love has to be earned; it doesn't just come naturally.

You will always love the person who gets up for you in the night when you have a bad dream, who holds your head and rubs your back when you are sick, and who comforts you when your love life is disastrous and tells you that there's plenty more fish in the sea. Also you will love a dad who gets up in the middle of the night to go into your cold bed when you have been out dancing so that you can get into his place and snuggle up to your mum.

I am now married to Stuart, who has been the love of my life and constant companion. When we did eventually marry, we changed the inscription on my mum and dad's headstone in the churchyard to include Stuart's name on it; I looked up towards heaven and said to them, 'Are you both happy now?'